All the material in this book was confirmed as accurate at the time of publication.

To all my Cornell girls—H.A.

To my wife, Leslye Moffat-Peña—J.M-P.

Text © 2023 Heather Alexander L.L.C. Illustrations © 2023 J. Moffat-Peña

First published in 2023 by Wide Eyed Editions, an imprint of The Quarto Group.
100 Cummings Center, Suite 265D, Beverly, MA 01915, USA.
T +1 978-282-9590 www.Quarto.com

A CIP record for this book is available from the Library of Congress.

ISBN 978-0-7112-8143-1
eBook ISBN 978-0-7112-8144-8

The illustrations were created digitally
Set in Quicksand and Thirsty Script

Designer: Myrto Dimitrakoulia
Editors: Hattie Grylls and Corinne Lucas
Production Controller: Dawn Cameron
Art Director: Karissa Santos
Publishers: Debbie Foy

Manufactured in Guangdong, China TT062023

9 8 7 6 5 4 3 2 1

FSC
www.fsc.org
MIX
Paper | Supporting
responsible forestry
FSC® C016973

Only in
NEW
YORK

Written by **Heather Alexander** · Illustrated by **J. Moffat-Peña**

WIDE EYED EDITIONS

Contents

Welcome to New York

Hop in the (imaginary) car, because we're heading on a wacky road trip to experience everything weird and wonderful this large, beautiful state has to offer. Uniquely New York (say that three times fast!) may be a tongue twister, but it's also a perfect description. We'll go from a loud, hustling-and-bustling city brimming with people from all over the world and buildings that touch the sky, to thick pine forests filled with hushed splendor and wondrous wildlife. We'll splash in ocean waves, lazy rivers, sparkling lakes, gorgeous gorges, and stare in awe at roaring waterfalls. As we travel, we'll keep an eye out for some of the offbeat, amazing, and just-plain-weird history, buildings, attractions, festivals, plants, animals, and people that make this state incredibly unique. With so much to do and see, it's no secret why everyone loves New York!

LAKE ONTARIO

NIAGARA FALLS

ROCHESTER

BUFFALO

LAKE ERIE

N W E S

The state's GEOGRAPHIC CENTER—an imaginary point—is believed to be in Pratts Hollow, just south of Oneida.

With the exception of Binghamton and Elmira, every major city falls along the trade route established by the ERIE CANAL.

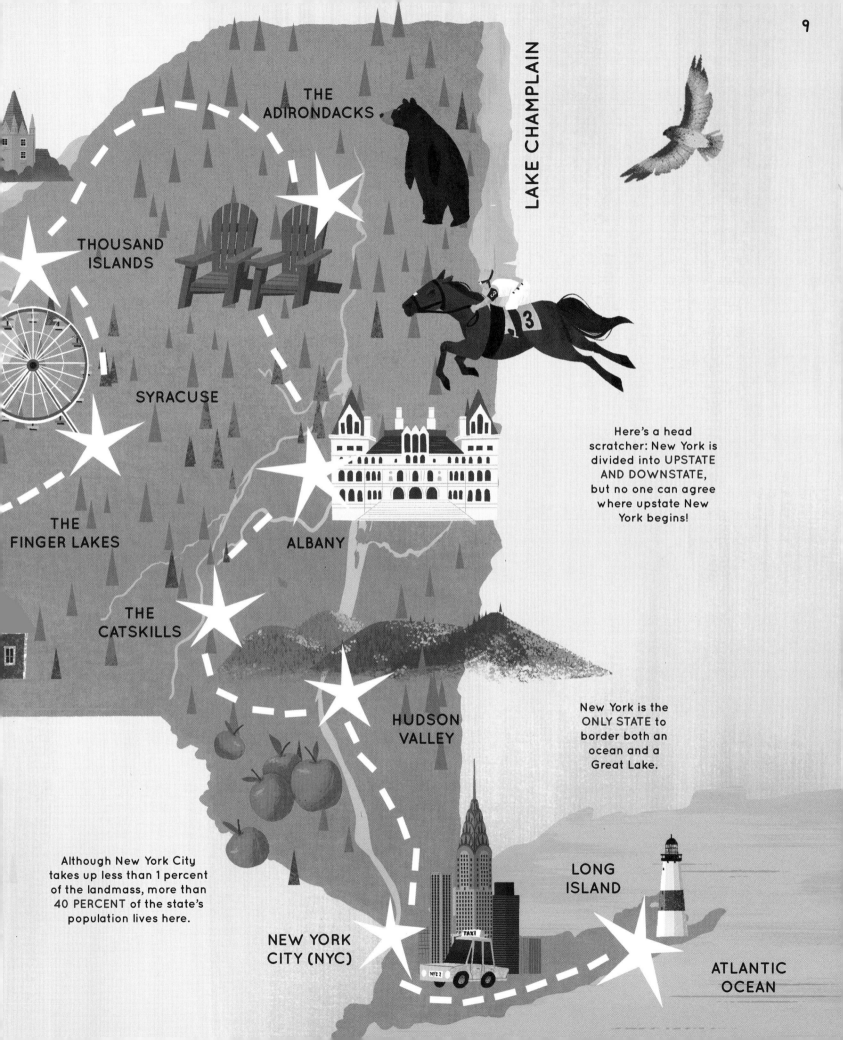

THE ADIRONDACKS

LAKE CHAMPLAIN

THOUSAND ISLANDS

SYRACUSE

THE FINGER LAKES

ALBANY

THE CATSKILLS

Here's a head scratcher: New York is divided into UPSTATE AND DOWNSTATE, but no one can agree where upstate New York begins!

HUDSON VALLEY

New York is the ONLY STATE to border both an ocean and a Great Lake.

Although New York City takes up less than 1 percent of the landmass, more than 40 PERCENT of the state's population lives here.

LONG ISLAND

NEW YORK CITY (NYC)

TAXI

NYC 2

ATLANTIC OCEAN

Stats & Facts

FAST FACTS

ABBREVIATION: NY

CAPITAL: Albany

STATEHOOD: July 26, 1788, 11th state

NUMBER OF COUNTIES: 62

POPULATION: Around 20 million, making it the fourth most populous state.

AREA: 54,555 square miles, making it the 27th largest state.

The STATE MOTTO, "Excelsior," is Latin for "Ever Upward." New Yorkers strive to do and be the best they can. Fun fact: "Excelsior!" was the catchphrase of Marvel Comics writer and publisher Stan Lee.

The STATE SLOGAN is "I Love New York." Well, there's no need to explain that!

In 1977, graphic artist Milton Glaser created the famous I ♥ NY LOGO while doodling on an envelope with a red crayon in the back of a taxi. The original sketch is at the Museum of Modern Art (MOMA) in NYC.

An unofficial nickname is the KNICKERBOCKER STATE. Knickerbockers, or "knickers," were pants rolled up to just-below-the-knee and worn by early Dutch settlers. In 1946, NYC's NBA basketball team took on the name, shortening it to the Knicks.

The state's nickname is the EMPIRE STATE. It might have come from George Washington, who once called New York "the Seat of the Empire," or it might refer to the state's many resources and wealth. What do you think?

Next-Door Neighbors
NORTH: Lake Ontario, Canada   **WEST:** Lake Erie, Canada

FANTASTIC NYC FIRSTS

- The first ICE CREAM PARLOR opened in NYC between 1776–1790.
- NYC was the FIRST CAPITAL of the United States under the U.S. Constitution from 1785 until 1790.
- The first STATE FAIR was held in Syracuse in 1841.
- The first passenger ELEVATOR was installed in NYC in 1857.
- The first amusement park ROLLER COASTER opened on Coney Island in 1884.
- Niagara Falls State Park became the first STATE PARK in 1885.
- The first PIZZERIA was started by an Italian immigrant in NYC in the 1890s.
- New York was the first state to require LICENSE PLATES on automobiles, in 1901.

STATE SUPERLATIVES

- NYC is the country's MOST POPULATED CITY. About one in every 38 people living in the United States lives here!
- The nation's TALLEST SKYSCRAPERS (as of 2023) are One World Trade Center (1,776 feet) and Central Park Tower (1,550 feet) in NYC.
- The world's LONGEST ELEVATED PEDESTRIAN BRIDGE connects Poughkeepsie and Highland.
- One of the nation's LARGEST FRESHWATER BEACHES is in Plattsburgh on Lake Champlain.
- Macy's at Herald Square in NYC is the nation's LARGEST DEPARTMENT STORE and host of one of the oldest THANKSGIVING DAY PARADES and the largest FOURTH OF JULY FIREWORKS celebration.
- Grand Central Terminal in NYC is the world's LARGEST TRAIN STATION by number of platforms (44).
- The nation's biggest NEW YEAR'S EVE PARTY features an annual ball drop in NYC's Times Square.
- NYC's Central Park is the country's MOST VISITED URBAN PARK.
- The George Washington Bridge connecting NYC to New Jersey is the BUSIEST BRIDGE in the world.

SOUTH: New Jersey, Pennsylvania, Atlantic Ocean   EAST: Connecticut, Massachusetts, Vermont

MANHATTAN IS AN ISLAND. Fifth Avenue is the dividing line between the east and west sides.

Completed in 1930, the CHRYSLER BUILDING was built in the art deco style to remind you of a shiny automobile. The building's decorative eagles and gargoyles represent the hood ornaments found on Chrysler cars at the time.

Fun fact: most BROADWAY THEATERS skip row "I" because many ticket holders would mistakenly sit in the first row.

People say there's one PIGEON for every person here. (It's likely a lot less.) These supersmart birds build their nests in the nooks and crannies of the city's tall buildings.

With a height-to-width ratio of 24:1, Steinway Tower is the world's MOST SLENDER SKYSCRAPER. It's also known as a pencil tower.

The STATUE OF LIBERTY wasn't always green. When it first arrived in New York Harbor, it was the color of a penny, but the air and water oxidized its copper exterior, turning it green.

Raise your hand to hail a TAXICAB. Most taxis are painted yellow—easy to spot from far away!

The SUBWAY system extends 665 miles and includes 472 stations. The tracks would stretch from NYC to Chicago if placed end to end!

The ANGEL OF THE WATERS statue at Bethesda Fountain in Central Park was the first public art commission awarded to a woman in NYC. Sculptor Emma Stebbins used her partner, actress Charlotte Cushman, as the model for the sculpture.

Manhattan

The antenna of the EMPIRE STATE BUILDING, the world's most photographed building, gets struck by lightning about 25 times each year. From the 102nd floor observation deck, you can see six states!

New York City

Start spreadin' the news—we're kicking off our quirky tour in one of the most exciting cities ever. NYC is a mosaic of cultures, with about 40 percent of New Yorkers born outside the U.S. and 800 different languages spoken here. With such a variety of people (lots of famous ones too) living so close together, something amazing happens every minute of every day! NYC is one city, but it's divided into five areas called boroughs: Manhattan, Queens, Brooklyn, the Bronx, and Staten Island. It's a good thing we're in the City That Never Sleeps—that gives us plenty of time to check them all out!

More movies are filmed along the winding paths of CENTRAL PARK than anywhere else in the world. The park has only one straight path!

Say "Hi" to the cat roaming the aisles when you stop at a neighborhood BODEGA, or small grocery shop. (There's always a cat!)

Get in line! STREET VENDORS from hundreds of countries feed hungry New Yorkers. Rice, salad, and halal meat with a squeeze of red or white sauce from halal carts is one of the most popular choices.

SENECA VILLAGE, a thriving pre-Civil War community of Black property owners, was torn down in 1857, uprooting 1,600 people, to make room for Central Park, the country's first landscaped public park.

Brooklyn

After the BROOKLYN BRIDGE opened in 1883, P. T. Barnum, the famous circus founder, paraded 21 elephants and 17 camels across it to show the strength of the world's first steel-wire suspension bridge.

Every Labor Day, the WEST INDIAN AMERICAN DAY PARADE dances down Eastern Parkway in a brightly colored display of culture and artistry.

When the country's first PASTA FACTORY opened in 1848 on the Brooklyn waterfront, spaghetti was often spread on the roof to dry in the sunshine.

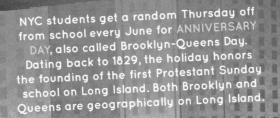

NYC students get a random Thursday off from school every June for ANNIVERSARY DAY, also called Brooklyn-Queens Day. Dating back to 1829, the holiday honors the founding of the first Protestant Sunday school on Long Island. Both Brooklyn and Queens are geographically on Long Island.

Queens

Called the "WORLD'S BOROUGH," Queens is one of the most culturally diverse places on the planet.

The UNISPHERE in Flushing Meadows Corona Park is an enormous model of Earth. Built for the 1964 World's Fair, the stainless steel globe was tricky to balance since Earth's continents aren't placed evenly.

Author Meg Medina, the first Latina to serve as NATIONAL AMBASSADOR FOR YOUNG PEOPLE'S LITERATURE, grew up in Flushing.

NYC has nine CHINATOWNS. Visit bustling Flushing for authentic xiao long bao, hot pot, boba, and egg custard tarts.

"Do, re, mi"! Many of the finest PIANOS in the world are made by hand at the Steinway & Sons factory in Astoria. (When you're in this neighborhood, be sure to try some Greek food!)

Staten Island

Called the "GREENEST BOROUGH," Staten Island has 170 parks!

The VERRAZZANO-NARROWS BRIDGE, connecting Staten Island and Brooklyn, was the world's longest suspension bridge when it opened in 1964.

The bright orange STATEN ISLAND FERRY took passengers to and from Lower Manhattan long before any bridges had been built. Five ferries run every day of the year, making over 100 trips in 24 hours!

DEPT. OF TRANSPORTATION

Staten Island Ferry

The Bronx

The Bronx is sometimes called *El Condado de la Salsa*, or "the borough of SALSA." The fast-paced, rhythmic melodies developed by Puerto Rican and Cuban musicians make everyone want to dance! The "Queen of Salsa," Celia Cruz, is buried at the Bronx's Woodlawn Cemetery.

You can smell tomato sauce and pizza strolling down ARTHUR AVENUE, often called the "real" Little Italy.

Go wild at the BRONX ZOO, one of the first zoos in the country with cage-free exhibits and an animal hospital. There are over 10,000 animals, representing more than 700 species.

HIP-HOP music came on the scene in 1973 at a block party in the Bronx, when Jamaican American DJ Clive "Kool Herc" Campbell used two turntables to extend the rhythmic section—or break—of a song.

History Timeline

Over 400 million years ago What is now the state of New York is submerged underwater. *Eurypterus remipes*, the official state fossil, was a giant sea scorpion.

1142 The Haudenosaunee Confederacy, made up of the Mohawks, Oneidas, Onondagas, Cayugas, and Senecas, unites the five Indigenous nations in the world's oldest participatory democracy. Each keeps its own identity. The Tuscarora join in 1722.

1524 Italian explorer Giovanni da Verrazzano sails into New York Harbor but soon goes back home.

1792 Stockbrokers meet under a buttonwood tree on Wall Street to set rules for trading securities. In 1817, what later becomes the New York Stock Exchange is created.

1788 New York ratifies the U.S. Constitution and becomes the 11th of the original 13 states to join the Union.

1776–1777 The Continental Army loses the Battle of Brooklyn, but then the British are defeated in the Battle of Saratoga, a turning point in the Revolutionary War.

1825 The Erie Canal opens. It begins at the Hudson River near Albany and ends more than 300 miles west in Lake Erie, near Buffalo.

1827 Slavery is abolished in New York. *Freedom's Journal*, published weekly from NYC, is the nation's first Black-owned and Black-operated newspaper.

1848 The nation's first women's rights convention is held in Seneca Falls. In 1917, New York passes an amendment for women's suffrage. The U.S. follows in 1920.

1952 The United Nations, an international peacekeeping organization, meets in its official NYC headquarters for the first time.

1945 Adam Clayton Powell Jr. becomes New York's first Black representative in the U.S. Congress.

1929 The New York Stock Exchange crashes, starting the Great Depression. About 15 million people lose their jobs!

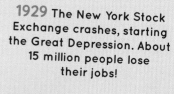

1969 Shirley Chisholm of Brooklyn becomes the first Black female representative in the U.S. Congress.

1969 The Woodstock music festival in upstate New York brings people together in the name of peace and love.

1980 In a surprising upset, the U.S. hockey team defeats the Soviet Union at the Winter Olympics in Lake Placid.

1984 New York is the first state to pass a mandatory seat belt law.

1609 English explorer Henry Hudson, employed by the Dutch, sails into New York Harbor and up a river in search of a route to present-day China. He doesn't find it—but the river does get his name.

1613 Juan Rodriguez, a Dominican sailor, is the first non-indigenous New Yorker. He remains to trap furs after his ship returns home.

1624 The Dutch set up a fur trading post in Fort Orange (present-day Albany) in the colony they named New Netherland. Two years later, they "buy" Manhattan Island from the Lenape Nation and call it New Amsterdam.

1653 Dutch leaders use enslaved labor to build a high wall to defend New Amsterdam. The wall is torn down in 1699, but Wall Street, the nation's financial district, keeps the name.

1776 As one of the original 13 colonies, New York signs the United States Declaration of Independence.

1690s The infamous pirate Captain Kidd makes NYC his home. After his death, some of his treasure is found on Long Island—and there may be more still hidden!

1664 British ships dock in New Amsterdam and demand the Dutch hand over the colony. And they do! No fight or anything. It's renamed for the king's brother, the Duke of York.

1883 The Brooklyn Bridge opens over the East River.

1885 The Statue of Liberty in New York Harbor is given as a gift from France ahead of the U.S.'s 100th birthday, or centennial, in 1886.

1871 Cuban-born Esteban Bellán is professional baseball's first Latin American player, starting for the Troy Haymakers.

1914 The Apollo Theater, where superstars such as Stevie Wonder, James Brown, Gladys Knight, and Billie Holiday will perform, opens in Harlem.

1904 NYC's subway system opens. A single ride costs 5 cents.

1892 Annie Moore, age 15 and from Ireland, is the first immigrant admitted into the U.S. through Ellis Island in New York Harbor. Some 12 million immigrants will travel through before it closes in 1954.

2001 The Twin Towers of the World Trade Center in NYC are destroyed by terrorists. Almost 3,000 people die.

2013 Grace Meng of Queens becomes the first Asian American from New York in the U.S. Congress.

2014 One World Trade Center opens on the site where the Twin Towers once stood. Reaching 1,776 feet tall (for the year the Declaration of Independence was signed), the skyscraper symbolizes the nation's strength and resilience.

2020 New York is an early epicenter of the COVID-19 pandemic. Healthcare heroes work tirelessly to help patients.

Say what? In 1985, the U.S. Supreme Court ruled that Long Island is a PENINSULA and not an island, even though it's surrounded by water on all sides. The court said the East River, separating Manhattan from Brooklyn and Queens, was too shallow for most ships to pass through, making Long Island a *legal* peninsula but a *geographical* island. Long Peninsula? We think not.

In 1958, physicist William Higinbotham created *Tennis for Two*, one of the FIRST VIDEO GAMES, as a way to entertain visitors to the Brookhaven National Laboratory.

Fire Island lighthouse is the state's TALLEST lighthouse.

JOHN PHILIP SOUSA, patriotic composer of "The Stars and Stripes Forever," lived in Sands Point. The brass sousaphone, a tuba used in marching bands, is named for him. What would an instrument named for you be called?

Climb 137 steps to the top of MONTAUK POINT LIGHTHOUSE. The state's oldest lighthouse has guided ships and submarines to safety for over 200 years.

The BELMONT STAKES on Long Island is the Triple Crown's longest horse race.

At the STRIPED BASS BLITZ each fall, the bait-filled waters overflow with "stripers," the state saltwater fish.

CHARLES LINDBERGH took off from Roosevelt Field in 1927 for his historic solo, nonstop flight across the Atlantic Ocean. His plane touched down in Paris, France, 33 hours and 30 minutes later. The same flight today takes just over seven hours.

The East End! MONTAUK POINT, the state's easternmost point, extends almost as far east as Rhode Island.

Splatter! In the 1950s, famous abstract expressionist painter JACKSON POLLOCK dripped paint onto large canvases placed on the floor of his home studio in East Hampton.

Old West in the East! Deep Hollow Ranch in Montauk claims to be the OLDEST CATTLE RANCH in the nation. Established in 1658, it's more than a century older than the U.S.!

Aw, shucks! The OYSTER FESTIVAL in Oyster Bay is one of the largest East Coast waterfront festivals. The slippery shellfish are filter feeders, naturally cleaning the bay and ocean waters.

While many species of SHARKS are found in Long Island's waters, including makos, blues, and threshers, the odds of being attacked by a shark are about one in four million.

Eye see you! The BAY SCALLOP have between 30 and 40 teeny-tiny eyes that work like telescopes, using natural mirrors to focus light. The scallop swims by opening and closing its fan-shaped shell, which happens to be the official state shell.

Long Island

From NYC, it doesn't take long to reach Long Island. Roll down the windows and inhale the salty air! Surrounded by the Atlantic Ocean and the Long Island Sound, Long Island boasts 118 miles of beachy awesomeness. No matter if you're on the North Shore or South Shore, the sand is always close by. Did you know that some people think Long Island is shaped like a fish? The North and South Forks (not the forks you use for eating, but the area where the island splits) make up the tail! Speaking of food ... let's head to the East End to gaze up at one of the 27 lighthouses and enjoy a scrumptious lobster roll for lunch.

Spectacular Sports

Baseball is the official state sport, and Cooperstown is home to the National Baseball Hall of Fame and Museum. Here you can view every World Series ring and also create a baseball card featuring YOU. But while New Yorkers sure love home runs, they can also be found enjoying so many different sports on the state's fields, courts, playgrounds, and tracks.

Can you name all the professional Empire State SPORTS TEAMS? See the last page of this book for a list of some of them.

High-octane speed! The Watkins Glen International, one of the country's fastest and most challenging road racing circuits, features both left and right turns. Most other NASCAR races have only left turns.

Each time a Mets player hits a home run at Citi Field, the HOME RUN APPLE sculpture pops up.

The LONGEST PROFESSIONAL BASEBALL GAME was between the Rochester Red Wings and the Pawtucket Red Sox. It lasted 33 innings, taking eight hours over two days to complete in 1981.

All you need to play HANDBALL is a small rubber ball, two people, and a wall. NYC has more than 2,000 outdoor courts.

In 1947, at Ebbets Field in Brooklyn, JACK (JACKIE) ROBINSON became the first Black athlete to play in a Major League Baseball game.

The New York Yankees have won the MOST WORLD SERIES and slugged the most home runs in baseball history.

LACROSSE, the country's oldest team sport, is believed to have been started by the Haudenosaunee in the 1100s, in what's now upstate New York. It was played on huge fields with about 1,000 players per side. Each game could last for days!

21

After champion tennis player BILLIE JEAN KING protested in 1973, the U.S. Open became the first tournament in any sport to award men and women equal prize money! Today, the tennis competition is held at Flushing Meadows Corona Park in Queens.

The NEW YORK CITY MARATHON, the world's largest 26.2-mile race, sprints through the five boroughs. At Mile 8 in Brooklyn, a high school marching band plays the *Rocky* theme song on repeat to energize the runners.

What's the most popular day of the year to hold a running race in the U.S.? Thanksgiving! Get your gobble on at Buffalo's TURKEY TROT, which is believed to be the nation's oldest continuous footrace, dating back to 1896.

Basketball games were slow and boring before Syracuse Nationals owner Danny Biasone invented the 24-SECOND SHOT CLOCK in 1954, limiting the time a player can hold on to the ball.

At the International Boxing Hall of Fame in Canastota, there's an actual BOXING RING from Madison Square Garden, with a bell you can chime!

George Franklin Grant, a dentist from Oswego, raised the ball when he invented the first WOODEN GOLF TEE in 1899.

Jump in! DOUBLE DUTCH got its name from the two long jump ropes that are twirled in opposite directions and from the early Dutch settlers who brought the ancient game with them to America. Double Dutch is a high school varsity sport in NYC.

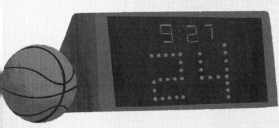

Giddyup! The SARATOGA RACE COURSE in Saratoga Springs is often called the Graveyard of Champions because so many famous racehorses have lost their race when running this track.

The lacy HUDSON RIVER WATER NYMPH plant is endemic to the area, meaning it grows only in the river's shallow waters and nowhere else on Earth.

BEEKMAN ARMS, established in 1766 in Rhinebeck, claims to be the nation's oldest inn.

Deborah Sampson was the country's FIRST FEMALE SOLDIER. Disguised as a man, she served in an elite Hudson Valley unit of the Continental Army during the Revolutionary War.

Gourd-ous! THE GREAT JACK O'LANTERN BLAZE at Van Cortlandt Manor in Croton-on-Hudson features more than 7,000 glowing, artist-carved pumpkins.

In 1999, a family in Hyde Park uncovered a skeleton of a MASTODON (an extinct relative of the elephant) in their backyard! It's now on display at the Museum of the Earth in Ithaca.

R.I.P. Fido! HARTSDALE PET CEMETERY, founded in 1896, is the country's oldest operating pet cemetery. More than 80,000 animals are buried here.

Hudson Valley

Boo! There's no better place for Halloween thrills and chills than the Hudson Valley. Every fall, this historic area is ablaze with golden-yellow, red, and orange leaves blowing in the crisp breeze. There's hot apple cider, sugar-covered donuts, corn mazes, farm stands piled high with pumpkins, and plenty of spine-tingling ghost stories. Washington Irving's fictional tale of the Headless Horseman (yep, a headless ghost riding a phantom horse) takes place in Sleepy Hollow, right on the banks of the river! Spook-tacular!

A floating SCIENCE BARGE in Yonkers has a sustainable hydroponics (a way to grow plants without soil) farm on board!

Soar above the Hudson River in an OPEN COCKPIT BIPLANE from the Old Rhinebeck Aerodrome.

Take a walk on the wild side! You can have an overnight campout with the wolves at the WOLF CONSERVATION CENTER in South Salem.

The Hudson River is about 315 MILES long and flows both north and south. The Lenape called it Mahicantuck, meaning "the river that runs both ways."

Storm King Art Center in New Windsor is the largest SCULPTURE PARK in the country.

The Hudson River is not just a river—it's a TIDAL ESTUARY. At high tide, salt water from the ocean combines with fresh water from the northern mountains.

In 1837, future-president MARTIN VAN BUREN was born in Kinderhook. He was the first president born in the U.S. and the first who spoke English as a second language—Dutch was his first.

A who's who of famous Black icons are buried at FERNCLIFF CEMETERY in Hartsdale, including Malcolm X, Betty Shabazz, Paul Robeson, Thelonious Monk, and James Baldwin.

George Washington realized the key to winning the Revolutionary War was blocking British ships from sailing up the Hudson River. Enter the great chain! He had a massive metal chain stretched from the WEST POINT area across the mighty river.

Trees & Flowers

Wood you believe that about 61 percent of the Empire State is covered by forests? While upstate New York boasts a strong plant game, it's not the only place bringing the green. About 700,000 trees line the streets of NYC —with more scheduled to take root soon.

Pass the pancakes! Only Vermont taps more SUGAR MAPLE trees for syrup than New York. Once winter's snow starts to melt, the trunk's sweet sap is collected, brought to a sugar shack, and boiled to make maple syrup.

Stop and smell the ROSES! The soft, fragrant petals of the official state flower are often used to make perfume.

The world's longest unbroken APPLE PEEL, created by 16-year-old Kathy Wafler Madison in Rochester in 1976, was 172 feet, 4 inches long.

New York grows enough APPLES each year to bake 500 million apple pies! McIntosh, Cortland, Red Delicious, and Empire are some of the most popular varieties. Fun fact: apples float because 25 percent of their volume is air!

DUTCHMAN'S BREECHES, found in the state's forests, have white and yellow flowers that look like tiny pairs of pantaloons hanging upside down on a clothesline.

The gnarled branches of the CAMPERDOWN ELM in Brooklyn's Prospect Park grow horizontal, or parallel, to the ground!

Twigs of the flowering DOGWOOD were chewed by Indigenous people to help whiten teeth.

When BEACH HEATHER blooms, it covers the Long Island sand dunes in a bright yellow blanket.

Every winter, since 1931, a towering NORWAY SPRUCE is chosen to be the Christmas tree in Manhattan's Rockefeller Center. After the holiday, the tree is milled into lumber then donated to Habitat for Humanity to build an affordable home.

Bees go a-buzz for the SERVICEBERRY tree's star-like white flowers, and birds gobble its tiny berries. You can eat them too! The berries taste like a mash-up of strawberry, blueberry, and almond.

Shoe-shaped flower! PINK LADY'S SLIPPERS, also known as moccasin flowers, are found in the Adirondack and Catskill forests. Nearly 60 species of wild orchids are native to New York.

The ALLEY POND GIANT, a tulip poplar tree in Queens, is believed to be 350 to 450 years old, making it one of the oldest trees in NYC.

The PAWPAW tree's fruit— green on the outside and creamy yellow on the inside— tastes like a mix of banana and mango.

Frankenstein tree! The TREE OF 40 FRUIT is one tree that magically grows 40 different types of stone fruit, including peaches, plums, apricots, cherries, and almonds. The hybrid was created by a Syracuse University professor who grafted, or joined together, branches from many trees.

Double trouble! KAATERSKILL FALLS is the tallest two-tiered waterfall in the state.

WOODSTOCK was a famous music festival, where nearly 500,000 "hippies" gathered in 1969 to promote peace and love. It was supposed to have been near Woodstock, but when that town didn't want it, Max Yasgur's son persuaded his dad to have the festival on their dairy farm in Bethel.

Outta sight! A grain silo in Mount Tremper was transformed into the world's largest KALEIDOSCOPE. Lie on the floor to gaze up at the ever-changing patterns made by light and mirrors.

Love to read? Turn the page in Hobart, a BOOK VILLAGE with seven bookstores but just 500 residents.

Hyde Hall Bridge in Cooperstown is the country's oldest COVERED BRIDGE. It was built in 1825.

New York's largest reported BLACK BEAR tipped the scales at about 750 pounds.

The Catskills

What's one of the coolest ways to experience the rolling hills of the Catskill Mountains? Zip line! So buckle up, hold on tight, and soar high above the treetops with us. Below you are the cozy river towns that attract and inspire all kinds of creative people, and hiking trails and ski runs cutting through the forested mountains. Everyone in the Catskills is busy enjoying the great outdoors. *Whoosh*—even the birds!

Stand in three different states on the TRI-STATE ROCK in Port Jervis! At the junction of the Delaware and Neversink Rivers, the rock is the official site where New York, New Jersey, and Pennsylvania meet.

The RED-TAILED HAWK has incredible eyesight. It can see four or five times farther than you and spot prey from great distances.

There are more than 100 Catskill peaks in the area, and 33 of them are over 3,500 feet high. Climb all 33 and you can join the CATSKILL 3500 CLUB.

The Catskills are not true mountains. Mountains are formed by forces that push up Earth's crust from below. Instead, these peaks are part of a DISSECTED PLATEAU known as the Allegheny Plateau. It's a plateau that's eroded and broken into smaller pieces.

THE GUNKS, the nickname for the Shawangunks Ridge, is one of the oldest and most popular rock-climbing areas in the country.

Logging competitions and raft races are at the center of the LUMBERJACK FESTIVAL in Deposit. How did the town get that name? Freshly cut logs were once "deposited" here to be floated down the Delaware River to market.

Museums & Attractions

Who's ready for tons of offbeat fun at quirky museums, thrilling amusement parks, and extremely curious exhibits? The Empire State is filled with so many unusual and awesome things to see and do!

There's a real Egyptian temple in the middle of NYC! You can step inside the Temple of Dendur at the METROPOLITAN MUSEUM OF ART (Met), as well as view more than two million pieces of art. The Met is the largest museum in the country!

Lie underneath a 94-foot-long model of an enormous blue whale at the AMERICAN MUSEUM OF NATURAL HISTORY in NYC, the largest natural history museum in the world.

Two World War II museums float on the Hudson River! A real aircraft carrier docked in NYC is home to the INTREPID SEA, AIR & SPACE MUSEUM, and the USS *Slater* moored in Albany houses the DESTROYER ESCORT HISTORICAL MUSEUM.

You can adopt your own wooden horse at the HERSCHELL CARROUSEL FACTORY MUSEUM in North Tonawanda, where most of the nation's merry-go-rounds were once built. (Think you spotted a typo? Nope! Herschell spelled *carousel* with a double *r*.)

Game time! Rochester's THE STRONG NATIONAL MUSEUM OF PLAY, the only museum in the world all about the "art of play," has the National Toy Hall of Fame and over 30,000 electronic games.

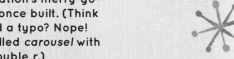

Try your hand at a bucket brigade at the FASNY MUSEUM OF FIREFIGHTING in Hudson. Did you know Molly Williams was the country's first-known female firefighter? She battled a blaze in NYC in 1818.

The electrifying and talented dancers of BALLET HISPÁNICO have celebrated Latinx culture on New York's stages for over 50 years!

Blown away! Watch a glob of goo turn into sparkling glass at the CORNING MUSEUM OF GLASS. Fun fact: the first light bulbs were blown by hand in Corning in the 1890s.

All aboard for the MEDINA RAILROAD MUSEUM, where there are hundreds of model historic trains. Then *chuga-chuga-choo-choo* across Lockport's Upside-Down Bridge!

Can you kazoo? The KAZOO MUSEUM in Eden lets you craft your own kazoo. The kazoo is a percussion instrument that you hum into.

What a scream! When the country's FIRST ROLLER COASTER opened on Coney Island's boardwalk in 1884, it went a whopping six miles per hour (yep, you can ride your bike faster!). Today, the famous wooden Cyclone roller coaster goes way faster.

When the BROOKLYN CHILDREN'S MUSEUM in Crown Heights opened in 1899, it was the world's first museum created just for kids.

KINGSTON was the first state capital before it moved to Albany in 1797.

The New York State Education Department building in Albany has 36 Corinthian columns, making it the longest COLONNADE in the country.

The Nott Memorial at Union College in Schenectady is one of the world's few 16-SIDED BUILDINGS. Fun fact: a polygon with 16 sides is called a hexadecagon or a hexakaidecagon.

Roll with it! Guptill's Arena in Cohoes is the world's largest INDOOR ROLLER-SKATING ARENA.

Founded in 1791, the ALBANY INSTITUTE OF HISTORY AND ART is among the country's oldest museums.

Four NEW YORK GOVERNORS went on to become President of the United States: Martin Van Buren, Grover Cleveland, Theodore Roosevelt, and Franklin D. Roosevelt. Five U.S. presidents were born in the state: Martin Van Buren, Millard Fillmore, Theodore Roosevelt, Franklin D. Roosevelt, and Donald J. Trump.

Scrub-a-dub-dub! The TULIP FESTIVAL, celebrating the city's Dutch heritage, begins with a scrubbing of State Street. In Washington Square Park, more than 140,000 tulips bloom in a rainbow of colors.

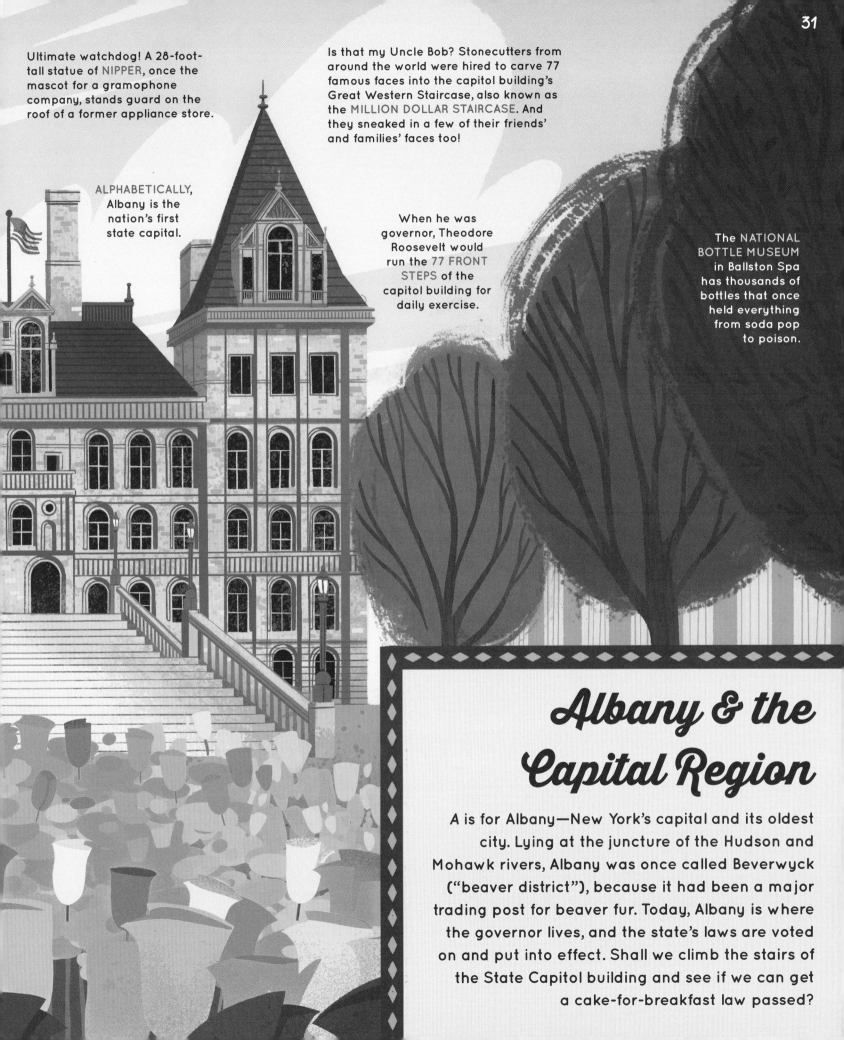

Ultimate watchdog! A 28-foot-tall statue of NIPPER, once the mascot for a gramophone company, stands guard on the roof of a former appliance store.

Is that my Uncle Bob? Stonecutters from around the world were hired to carve 77 famous faces into the capitol building's Great Western Staircase, also known as the MILLION DOLLAR STAIRCASE. And they sneaked in a few of their friends' and families' faces too!

ALPHABETICALLY, Albany is the nation's first state capital.

When he was governor, Theodore Roosevelt would run the 77 FRONT STEPS of the capitol building for daily exercise.

The NATIONAL BOTTLE MUSEUM in Ballston Spa has thousands of bottles that once held everything from soda pop to poison.

Albany & the Capital Region

A is for Albany—New York's capital and its oldest city. Lying at the juncture of the Hudson and Mohawk rivers, Albany was once called Beverwyck ("beaver district"), because it had been a major trading post for beaver fur. Today, Albany is where the governor lives, and the state's laws are voted on and put into effect. Shall we climb the stairs of the State Capitol building and see if we can get a cake-for-breakfast law passed?

Food, Glorious Food

Delight your taste buds with delicious empire eats and tasty treats from all around the state.

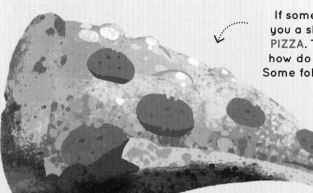

If someone in NYC offers you a slice, they're talking PIZZA. The big question is how do you eat your slice? Some fold it and some don't.

ENGLISH MUFFINS aren't from England! They were invented in NYC in 1880 by Englishman Samuel Bath Thomas and first called "toaster crumpets." Supposedly, only seven people in the world know his top-secret recipe.

One night in 1964, when the owner of Anchor Bar in Buffalo needed to feed his hungry friends, his mom came to the rescue. She fried chicken wings, tossed them in peppery hot sauce, and served them with blue cheese and celery. BUFFALO WINGS were a hit!

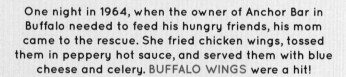

In Albany, gooey fried mozzarella sticks are dipped in raspberry MELBA SAUCE, named for Australian opera singer Nellie Melba.

Binghamton's SPIEDIES (pronounced spee-dies) are marinated cubes of meat grilled on a skewer and served in a hoagie roll or on Italian bread. The Italian word *spiedino* means "skewer."

BAGEL 'N' LOX is mash-up magic! One hundred years ago, Eastern European Jewish immigrants living in NYC's Lower East Side combined bagels from Poland, salty lox (cured salmon) from Scandinavia, and a schmear of New York cream cheese for the perfect breakfast. Some say the city's water makes bagels here taste so great.

New York produces more Greek yogurt than Greece! Thanks to fourth graders from Bergen, YOGURT is the state snack.

Which came first: NYC's black and white cookies or Central New York's half moon cookie? No one knows. But both CAKE-LIKE COOKIES are double the yum. Which do you prefer? We'll eat both while you decide!

While not invented here (it's believed to have been served to athletes at the first Olympic Games in ancient Greece!), CHEESECAKE became a NYC favorite after Jewish bakers added cream cheese to the recipe.

TOMATO PIE isn't quite pizza or a pie, but it sure is delicious! Enjoy the focaccia topped with zesty tomato sauce and a sprinkle of Romano cheese in Utica and Rome.

Utica cooks up CHICKEN RIGGIES (rhymes with "piggies")—chicken, rigatoni, and hot peppers in a spicy pink cream sauce.

Can you guess what's in Rochester's GARBAGE PLATE? A lot! Heaps of home fries, french fries, baked beans, macaroni salad, cheeseburgers, and hot dogs (or whatever other meat you desire) topped with meat sauce, onions, and yellow mustard. Oh, and there's buttered bread on the side!

Soak up sweetness with Buffalo's favorite SPONGE CANDY, a crunchy, air-bubble-filled toffee covered in chocolate.

Take a big bite of the classic NYC deli sandwich PASTRAMI ON RYE with mustard. Seasoned and smoked pastrami, which hailed from Romania, was a way to preserve meat without a refrigerator in the 1800s.

CHICKEN FRENCH or chicken francese, another Rochester favorite, has fried chicken cutlets swimming in a lemony butter sauce.

• Coney Island is the birthplace of the AMERICAN HOT DOG, served with spicy brown mustard, relish, and sauerkraut.
• Nathan's Famous hosts an annual Fourth of July HOT DOG EATING CONTEST!
• The Capital Region has MINI-DOGS, a "litter" of tiny hot dogs topped with yellow mustard and chopped onions.
• Western New York's snapping WHITE HOTS aren't smoked or cured, so the meat looks white.
• Plattsburgh grills up MICHIGANS, or meat-slathered hot dogs.

Thousand Islands

Water, water everywhere . . . and islands galore! The gleaming St. Lawrence River is home to the Thousand Islands, but whoever came up with the name needs a counting lesson, because there are actually 1,864 islands. Some islands are big, with cottages and stores, and some are tiny, with just a single tree. Some islands are in New York, and some are in Canada. The St. Lawrence River creates a zigzagging international border, but it's smooth sailing to view glorious pine forests, beaches, and castles. Yep, castles. Over one hundred years ago, some millionaires built island castles here!

Where do you think the creamy pink THOUSAND ISLAND DRESSING was created? Oh, you're so smart!

The Thousand Islands are an ARCHIPELAGO—a fancy name for a chain or group of islands scattered close together.

To be an official ISLAND here (and not just a big rock), a piece of land must stay above water 365 days a year, be larger than one square foot, and have at least one living tree or shrub on it.

The river is a nonstop parade of boats. SALTIES are huge ocean-going freighters that arrive from overseas on the St. Lawrence Seaway.

Do some of the many old SHIPWRECKS at the bottom of the river contain underwater treasure? Did pirates bury gold and jewels on some islands? Many folks think so. Time for a treasure hunt!

BEAVERS, the state mammal, have orange teeth because of the iron in their enamel. Their teeth never stop growing, so they chew on branches to file them down.

The world's smallest inhabited island is called JUST ROOM ENOUGH ISLAND. There's only space for a family's small cottage. And a tree.

In 1900, wealthy hotel owner George Boldt began building BOLDT CASTLE for his wife. It has 120 rooms, a bowling alley, tunnels, a pool, and even a drawbridge. But when she died in 1904, he stopped construction and refused to ever go back. The castle sat empty for 73 years before it was finally finished.

SINGER CASTLE on Dark Island was designed to look like a Scottish castle. Its library has a secret door opened by a switch hidden in a book, and a framed portrait lets someone hiding inside the walls spy on unknowing guests.

Sleek St. Lawrence River skiffs are on display at Clayton's ANTIQUE BOAT MUSEUM, the world's largest freshwater maritime museum.

The DOUBLE-CRESTED CORMORANT's turquoise eyes match the inside of its mouth! Its feathers aren't waterproof, so this deep-diving water bird dries them by standing still like a statue with its wings open.

DR. MARY WALKER of Oswego, a Civil War surgeon, is the only woman to have ever been awarded the military's Medal of Honor. She crossed enemy lines to care for suffering civilians.

Fish on! Reeling in giant MUSKIES (muskellunge) is hard work, because "the fish of 10,000 casts" are awesome at dodging fishhooks. Lately, there are fewer in the river because the invasive round goby fish are eating their eggs.

Amazing Animals

With the state's incredibly diverse animal species, it's easy to witness wildlife in action from trails to trees, sidewalks to seashore, and even in your very own backyard.

The BOBCAT, found across roughly a quarter of the state, looks like a very large house cat but with a short bobbed tail. They're crepuscular (active at dusk and dawn), sneaking up on prey, then . . . pouncing!

Known for their long eyestalks and white claws, GHOST CRABS can change color to blend in with the sand. They hunt at night on Long Island beaches.

The world's largest herd of ALL-WHITE WHITE-TAILED DEER, usually easy prey for predators and hunters because of their color, are protected at the Deer Haven Park wildlife sanctuary in Romulus.

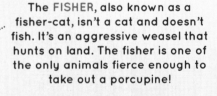

The FISHER, also known as a fisher-cat, isn't a cat and doesn't fish. It's an aggressive weasel that hunts on land. The fisher is one of the only animals fierce enough to take out a porcupine!

Unlike other turtle species, the COMMON SNAPPING TURTLE, the state reptile, can't hide in its shell when threatened. It uses its powerful jaw to defend itself instead.

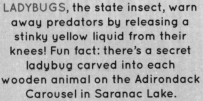

LADYBUGS, the state insect, warn away predators by releasing a stinky yellow liquid from their knees! Fun fact: there's a secret ladybug carved into each wooden animal on the Adirondack Carousel in Saranac Lake.

The male EASTERN BLUEBIRD, the state bird, can sing with its beak closed!

The nocturnal WHIP-POOR-WILL bird is named after its call and has an extra-large mouth perfect for catching moths and large insects at night.

Picky eater! The endangered KARNER BLUE BUTTERFLY, found in the Albany Pine Bush Preserve, eats only the leaves of the wild blue lupine.

Ultimate fake-out! If the EASTERN GRAY SQUIRREL notices another squirrel, or even a human, watching it bury a nut, it will *pretend* to bury it but then secretly hide the nut somewhere else.

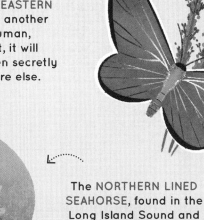

The NORTHERN LINED SEAHORSE, found in the Long Island Sound and Hudson River, uses its long tail to help stay upright and cling to underwater eelgrass.

Ouch! A PORCUPINE's body is covered with around 30,000 hollow, needle-sharp quills. The prickly rodent's name means "quill pig" in Latin.

A RACCOON'S five-finger front paws look a lot like human hands, letting them grasp, rip, twist, and turn stuff. They can also lift garbage-can lids to scavenge food.

Fetch! Finley Molloy, a GOLDEN RETRIEVER from Canandaigua, carried a record-breaking six tennis balls in his mouth at one time!

GOATS in Gotham! Several goats spend summers in NYC's Riverside Park eating invasive plants to avoid the need for chemical herbicides. Did you know that the NYC nickname "Gotham", which means "goat's town" in Old English, was originally a put down?

Rise up! Take the elevator to the top of the 120-meter (394-foot) Olympic SKI JUMP in Lake Placid to watch skiers zoom down the ramp and launch into the air.

The name "46ers" is given to people who have climbed all 46 HIGH PEAKS. Dogs love climbing too! The first recorded canine to summit all 46 was named Chrissie.

In 1901, Vice President Theodore Roosevelt was hiking MOUNT MARCY, the state's highest peak (5,344 feet above sea level), when he learned the president had died. Roosevelt had to race down the mountain and across the state to be sworn in as president!

The majestic and mysterious moose calls these forests home. Compete in the moose calling contest at the GREAT ADIRONDACK MOOSE FESTIVAL in Indian Lake.

AUSABLE CHASM is a 150-foot-deep gorge made out of 500-million-year-old sandstone.

Where was the comfy ADIRONDACK CHAIR invented? Yep, it was here! Relax into one of the gigantic, oversized chairs dotting the roadways from Lake George to Lake Placid.

Get cozy inside a larger-than-life BALD EAGLE'S NEST high above the treetops at The Wild Center in Tupper Lake.

Forever wild! The Adirondack Mountains are over one billion years old and still GETTING TALLER, growing up to an eighth of an inch each year, or one foot every hundred years.

The Cliffside Coaster at Mount Van Hoevenberg claims to be the LONGEST MOUNTAIN COASTER in North America. It twists and turns along the heart-pounding track once used by the 1932 and 1980 Olympic bobsledders.

The Adirondacks

Adventure awaits in the Adirondack Mountains! Called North Country because it's pretty much the farthest north in the state we can go, the 'Dacks are all about endless wilderness and natural beauty. And we mean endless! Spanning more than six million acres, Adirondack Park is larger than Yellowstone, Yosemite, Grand Canyon, Glacier, and Olympic parks combined! So what's it going to be? Swimming in or skating over glassy lakes? Hiking or skiing on majestic mountains? Daydreaming on a dock? Roasting marshmallows over a campfire? Let's do it all!

Cast a line into the clear, cool lakes to reel in a *brookie*, a nickname for the BROOK TROUT. Here's something fishy: the state's freshwater fish is really a char, not a trout.

Shiny dark-red GARNET, the state gem, is found in Barton Mines. When crushed, garnet is used in sandpaper.

If you see someone doing the "Adirondack wave," or frantically swatting the air around them, it must be BLACK FLY SEASON. From the middle of May through early July, swarms of the pesky insects descend. Only female black flies do the biting.

The NORTH STAR UNDERGROUND RAILROAD MUSEUM in Chesterfield tells the story of how enslaved people seeking freedom in the 1800s passed through the region on the way to Canada.

LAKE PLACID is the only U.S. city to host the Winter Olympics twice—in 1932 and in 1980.

Cool Inventions

New Yorkers eagerly embrace the new, incredible, and never-been-seen-before. So many firsts happened in the Empire State, because if you can make it here, you can make it anywhere!

CAMERAS used to be as big as microwave ovens and required glass plates and messy chemicals to take a photograph. Enter George Eastman of Rochester. In the 1880s, he invented roll film and the handheld, push-button camera.

Legend has it the POTATO CHIP was invented in Saratoga Springs in 1853. A restaurant customer complained about his French fries. Chef George Crum was annoyed, so he cut the potatoes super thin, extra-fried them, and overloaded them with salt. The customer loved them! Another version of the story has the chef's sister, Kate Wicks, accidentally dropping a potato slice into oil.

Chester dairy farmer William Lawrence invented CREAM CHEESE when he added cream to Neufchâtel cheese in the 1870s. It was sold as "Philadelphia Brand," because Philly had a superior cheese reputation at the time. Spread the fun on thick at Lowville's annual CREAM CHEESE FESTIVAL.

When Joseph C. Gayetty of NYC produced the first packaged TOILET PAPER in 1857, it wasn't a success. Although people in China had been using toilet paper for centuries, most Americans thought it was a waste of money when they could wipe with leaves, corncobs, or magazines!

In 1897, Pearle Bixby Wait was experimenting with making cough syrup at home and accidentally concocted a fruit-flavored jiggly gelatin dessert. His wife named it JELL-O. Stop by the Jell-O Gallery Museum in Le Roy for more sweet trivia.

When you crank up the AIR-CONDITIONING on a sweltering summer day, thank Willis Carrier from Buffalo. In 1902, he designed the "Apparatus for Treating Air," which later became the modern air-conditioning unit.

Snow what? Carl Frink of Clayton designed one of the first car-mounted SNOWPLOWS in 1920.

35TH AVENUE

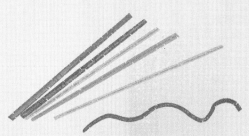

Poughkeepsie native Alfred M. Butts invented the board game SCRABBLE in the 1930s in Queens. Today there's a street sign in Queens written in the game's letter-scoring system.

The CHICKEN NUGGET wasn't created in someone's kitchen, but in a Cornell University laboratory in 1963 by agricultural science professor Robert C. Baker.

John Harry Stedman and Charles Angel invented chenille PIPE CLEANERS in the early 1900s to, you guessed it, clean tobacco pipes. Today, we twist 'em into fabulous craft projects.

Dr. Patricia Bath, an ophthalmologist (eye doctor) from Harlem, was the first Black female doctor to receive a patent for a medical invention. In 1986, she invented the LASERPHACO PROBE, a laser device to remove cataract lenses from eyes.

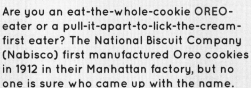

When Tom Carvel's ice-cream truck got a flat tire in Hartsdale on a hot day in 1934, he sold his melting ice cream to people driving by. It was a light bulb moment! He then created the first SOFT-SERVE ICE CREAM machine.

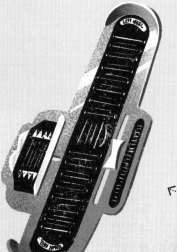

At some time or other, you've probably put your foot in a BRANNOCK DEVICE. Charles F. Brannock was a student at Syracuse University in 1926 when he invented a metal tool for shoe stores to properly measure feet. During World War II, the U.S. Army used it to fit soldiers for combat boots.

Are you an eat-the-whole-cookie OREO-eater or a pull-it-apart-to-lick-the-cream-first eater? The National Biscuit Company (Nabisco) first manufactured Oreo cookies in 1912 in their Manhattan factory, but no one is sure who came up with the name.

Jacob Myers of Rochester created a VOTING MACHINE with a mechanical lever and a privacy curtain, making voting faster (no more paper ballots to count by hand) and more honest. First used in Lockport in 1892, the lever voting machine continued until computers took over in the 1990s.

VOTE HERE

The TOOTSIE ROLL, invented by Brooklyn candymaker Leo Hirschfield in 1896, was the first penny candy sold individually wrapped. Goodbye, grubby hands in candy jars! According to company lore, "Tootsie" was his daughter's nickname.

Syracuse & Central New York

We're hanging up here on the Ferris wheel at the Great New York State Fair in Syracuse 'cause the splendiferous views of Central New York's hilly farmland do not disappoint. Syracuse has been home to the end-of-summer fair since 1841, making this the oldest state fair in the country. Crowds fill the fairgrounds, eager to play midway games, pet cute animal babies, gasp at the enormous sand sculptures, and eat food on a stick and cotton candy. Okay, we're smelling barbecue and potatoes . . . It's time to go down and join the fun!

Wear your kilt for Highland dancing, piping, and drumming at the Central New York SCOTTISH GAMES AND CELTIC FESTIVAL.

Eat your greens! UTICA GREENS are a garlicky Italian American side dish made with escarole, hot peppers, and bread crumbs.

"I've got a mule and her name is Sal" begins the famous "Erie Canal" song. Mules were chosen to pull boats along the waterway because they're smart and fast and needed less food and water than horses. Learn more at Syracuse's ERIE CANAL MUSEUM.

Syracuse's Tipperary Hill neighborhood has the world's only known UPSIDE-DOWN TRAFFIC LIGHT. Many Irish immigrants lived here in the 1920s and, because of anti-British sentiment, they put the green light (Ireland) above the red light (Britain).

In 2019, more people went to the NEW YORK STATE FAIR than lived in Montana. If everyone at the fair held hands, the people chain would stretch from Syracuse to Orlando, Florida!

Nicknamed SALT CITY, Syracuse was once the country's main salt producer. Visit the Salt Museum to learn how the Onondaga Nation and then European settlers boiled brine from springs near Onondaga Lake to produce salt.

Every year, the fair displays an 800-POUND BUTTER SCULPTURE. You *butter* believe that's a lot of butter! It would take the average person about 127 years to eat that much butter on their own! After the fair, the butter is recycled into renewable energy.

The CARRIER DOME, the country's largest basketball arena, is a sea of orange as fans cheer for the Syracuse Orange. Otto the Orange is a mascot with "a-peel"!

So salty! Each year at the fair, more than 34,000 pounds of SALT POTATOES—small, round potatoes boiled in tons of salt—are sold. That's more than the weight of eight cars!

Chow down on platters of ribs and brisket at the legendary DINOSAUR BAR-B-QUE. Each smoker, where the meat is cooked over low heat, is given a name.

In 1992, a librarian in Liverpool named Jean Armour Polly created the phrase SURFING THE INTERNET to show that using computers was fun but required skill . . . like surfing the waves!

Fun Festivals

The spirit of New York is loud and proud at festivals that are wacky, incredible, and often mind-blowing! From pickle juice to canine costumes, there's something for everyone.

Watch ginormous balloons get inflated in the streets of NYC's Upper West Side the night before the MACY'S THANKSGIVING DAY PARADE.

The first NYC ST. PATRICK'S DAY PARADE celebrating Irish culture was held 14 years before the signing of the Declaration of Independence.

GOBBLE

GOBBLE

One wheel is better than two when the NYC UNICYCLE FESTIVAL rolls into town. Got game? Play unicycle basketball!

Gobble-gobble! Compete in the turkey-calling contest for kids at the STEUBEN COUNTY FAIR in Bath, the country's longest continuously running county fair.

Celebrate the town that was once one of the world's largest producers of sauerkraut with cabbage bowling at Phelps SAUERKRAUT WEEKEND. Sauerkraut is made from fermented cabbage.

So cool! The Ice Palace at the SARANAC LAKE WINTER CARNIVAL is made from thousands of two-ton ice blocks cut from Lake Flower.

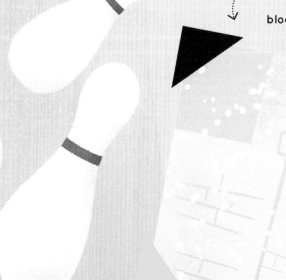

At the HUDSON VALLEY GARLIC FESTIVAL in Saugerties, try garlic soup and garlic ice cream.

Paddle fast at Lake Henry's CHAMP DAY Cardboard Boat Race 'cause Champ, the legendary lake monster, is said to live in the waters of Lake Champlain.

The ROSENDALE INTERNATIONAL PICKLE FESTIVAL is a big *dill*! Pucker up for the pickle-juice-drinking, pickle-eating, and pickle-toss triathlon competition.

Joy fills Fifth Avenue in NYC during the NATIONAL PUERTO RICAN DAY PARADE, the country's largest cultural celebration.

Will your favorite breed win Best in Show at the annual WESTMINSTER KENNEL CLUB DOG SHOW? The winning pooch is treated to a fancy lunch on a silver platter at Sardi's restaurant in NYC. Yum!

Cuteness overload! The Tompkins Square HALLOWEEN DOG PARADE in NYC is the world's biggest dog costume parade.

Talk about messy! At the NATIONAL BUFFALO CHICKEN WING FESTIVAL in Buffalo, bob for wings in a baby pool filled with blue cheese dressing.

THE FINGER LAKES (from west to east) are named after different Indigenous nations: Conesus, Hemlock, Canadice, Honeoye, Canandaigua, Keuka, Seneca, Cayuga, Owasco, Skaneateles, and Otisco. Cayuga Lake is the longest. Seneca Lake is the deepest. Everyone has a favorite lake. Which is yours?

GANONDAGAN in Victor was once the site of a vibrant Seneca village in the 1600s. Tour the Bark Longhouse to experience how Seneca families used to live.

TAUGHANNOCK FALLS in Ithaca is the state's highest waterfall—25 feet higher than the American side of Niagara Falls.

The statue of famed orator and abolitionist FREDERICK DOUGLASS in Rochester was the first statue in the country to honor a Black American.

HORSEHEADS is the nation's only village dedicated to the service of the American military horse.

Do fairies inhabit the teeny-tiny houses along the FAIRY TRAIL in Mendon Ponds Park in Rochester? No one knows who put the houses there!

In 1916, brothers John and Walter Wegman began selling vegetables from a horse-drawn wagon in Rochester. This eventually became WEGMANS SUPERMARKETS. Fun fact: Wegmans has cheese caves where cheese is stored to age and ripen.

The Finger Lakes & Rochester

Want to guess how the Finger Lakes got their name? Yep, they do look like the long, slender fingers of a hand! Well, that's assuming there's a hand somewhere with 11 fingers on it, since there are 11 lakes. We've got to hand it to the Ice Age glaciers for sculpting such splendid sparkling lakes and hundreds of gorgeous gorges and waterfalls. Along with all the fields, forests, and many, many farms, the west-central part of the state is oh so *hand*some!

Keuka Lake, nicknamed the CROOKED LAKE, is shaped like a Y. It's the only lake in the country that flows both north and south.

Whoooo goes there? The GREAT HORNED OWL doesn't have horns. Its name comes from the two tufts of feathers on its head that look like horns.

Rochester's annual DEAF FESTIVAL celebrates one of the nation's largest populations of deaf and hard-of-hearing people.

Looking for the Grand Canyon of the East? Visit LETCHWORTH STATE PARK, which has the nation's first nature trail specifically designed for visitors on the autism spectrum.

Celebrate the Concord grape harvest with a purplicious GRAPE PIE-eating contest at the Naples Grape Festival. The town even has purple fire hydrants!

Once nicknamed FLOUR CITY because of flour mills powered by the Genesee River, Rochester is now called Flower City. Highland Park has the country's largest collection of LILACS, the official state bush, and a big Lilac Festival every May.

Change Makers

Countless creative and courageous New Yorkers have transformed our world. Here are just a handful of influential pioneers, artists, authors, activists, athletes, and leaders. Many were the first from their community to achieve a goal, effect change, or do something super cool.

SUSAN B. ANTHONY led the fight that successfully granted U.S. women's suffrage, or the right to vote. After growing up in Battenville and Rochester, she and Elizabeth Cady Stanton founded the National Woman Suffrage Association in 1869. She died before the law was changed, but her work is remembered with the Susan B. Anthony Dollar, making her the first woman to appear on a circulating U.S. coin.

Raised in the Bronx, LIN-MANUEL MIRANDA is an actor, writer, singer, and songwriter who created and starred in the blockbuster Broadway musicals *In the Heights* and *Hamilton* and composed music for the movies *Encanto* and *Moana*. After reading a book about Alexander Hamilton, the first Secretary of the Treasury, Miranda got the idea to turn Hamilton's life into a musical that blended rap, hip-hop, and salsa.

In 2009, SONIA SOTOMAYOR became the first Hispanic and first Latina to be appointed a Supreme Court justice. Born in the Bronx to parents from Puerto Rico, she always loved to read and has said managing her diabetes as a kid taught her discipline. She worked as a lawyer before being appointed a judge.

JONAS SALK was a doctor and scientist from NYC who, along with Dr. Julius Youngner, Major Byron L. Bennett, and Dr. L. James Lewis, developed one of the first vaccines for polio, an infectious disease. Salk believed that if the polio virus was killed with a chemical, then injected into human bodies, we would develop defenses against it. And he was right! Today polio is almost completely gone worldwide.

In 1968, Brooklyn-born SHIRLEY CHISHOLM became the first Black woman elected to U.S. Congress. She served for 14 years and was a champion of the working class and education. In 1972, Chisholm became the first Black woman to run for U.S. president. Her slogan was "Unbought and Unbossed." She didn't get the nomination but, after she died, she was awarded the Presidential Medal of Freedom.

LUCILLE BALL was told by her teachers she was too shy to be an actress. The Jamestown native sure proved them wrong! Known for her laugh-out-loud show *I Love Lucy*, Ball was the first woman to run a major Hollywood studio; she and Desi Arnaz, her Cuban American husband, were TV's first interracial couple; and she was the first pregnant actress to play a pregnant woman on TV.

After escaping enslavement herself, HARRIET TUBMAN took the dangerous trip back down south about 13 times to secretly lead around 70 freedom seekers north. She was such an excellent guide on the Underground Railroad that she was often called Moses. She also served in the Civil War as a nurse and spy, and then spent the rest of her life working for human rights and dignity. You can visit her home in Auburn.

Comic-book creator STAN LEE, along with fellow NYC native Jack Kirby, gave the world the Fantastic Four, Spider-Man, the Hulk, Iron Man, Doctor Strange, the X-Men, and other iconic superheroes. Born Stanley Lieber, he became publisher of Marvel Comics and changed comic books by creating imperfect superheroes and tackling real-world issues in his stories.

MABEL PING-HUA LEE was an activist who campaigned for women's right to vote. In 1912, at age 16, she led a historic parade of thousands of suffragist marchers. But when the 19th Amendment passed, Lee still couldn't vote because the Chinese Exclusion Act prohibited Chinese immigrants from becoming citizens (it was repealed in 1943). She continued to fight for women as a Baptist minister and community activist in NYC's Chinatown.

The paintings of Brooklyn-born artist JEAN-MICHEL BASQUIAT may seem simple at first, but look closer to spot his deeper messages about our world and nods to African, Caribbean, Aztec, and Hispanic cultures. He started off doing street graffiti and, by his twenties, Basquiat was making paintings that would later sell for $110 million! His painting style is called neo-expressionism.

In 1993, Brooklyn native RUTH BADER GINSBURG became the first Jewish person and second woman to be named Supreme Court justice. RBG was one of the first women admitted to Harvard Law School and later co-founded the Women's Rights Project for the American Civil Liberties Union and was never afraid to disagree when she believed something was unfair.

One of the first true sports superstars, BABE RUTH is considered the most famous baseball player ever. Wearing the New York Yankees pinstripes, he changed the game by hitting 714 career home runs (1914–1935) and tallying a .690 lifetime slugging percentage! The former Yankee Stadium was called "the House that Ruth Built."

Born in Puerto Rico in 1903, PURA BELPRÉ became the first Puerto Rican librarian in the New York Public Library system. Belpré was also the first librarian to travel all over the city telling stories in both Spanish and English. And when she couldn't find any books for kids written in Spanish, she wrote one herself! Her folktale about a cockroach and a mouse was part of the first Spanish-language children's book published by a mainstream U.S. press.

50

Go for gold with the Olympic sport CURLING—it's like shuffleboard, except you use brooms to move heavy stones along the ice.

HOT COCOA

Hit the ice! HOCKEY PUCKS are often frozen to prevent them from bouncing during games.

Is it a shark? Is it a girl? SHARK GIRL is a piece of public art! She's always happy to take a selfie with you.

Two U.S. PRESIDENTS, Millard Fillmore and Grover Cleveland, were from Buffalo. In 1901, President William McKinley was assassinated while visiting the city.

When temperatures drop, grab an ice-cycle. With blades instead of wheels, ICE BIKES let you pedal across frozen water.

Buffalo has two BRAIN MUSEUMS, with almost 90 brains in one and about 40 in the other! Located on the University of Buffalo campuses, they're the only museums in the country dedicated exclusively to the brain.

Why does the city smell like CHEERIOS? General Mills bakes the breakfast cereal every day in its factory on the Buffalo River, and the winds carry the aroma around the city.

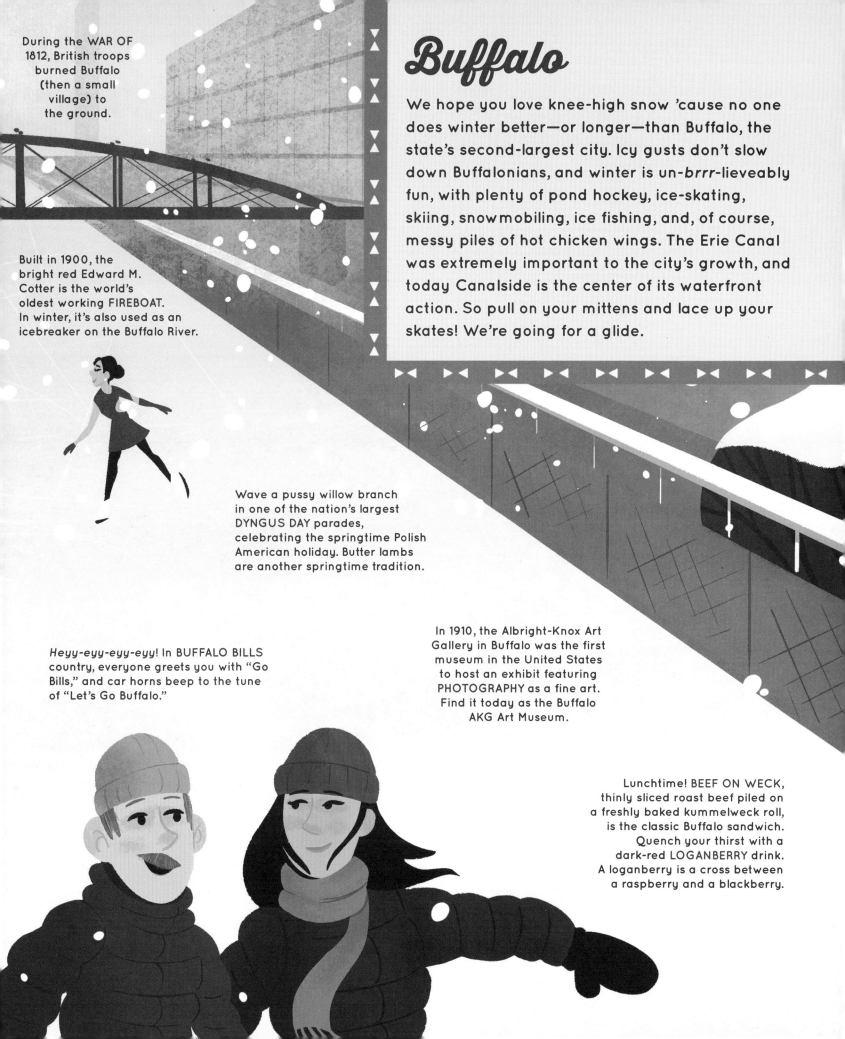

During the WAR OF 1812, British troops burned Buffalo (then a small village) to the ground.

Built in 1900, the bright red Edward M. Cotter is the world's oldest working FIREBOAT. In winter, it's also used as an icebreaker on the Buffalo River.

Buffalo

We hope you love knee-high snow 'cause no one does winter better—or longer—than Buffalo, the state's second-largest city. Icy gusts don't slow down Buffalonians, and winter is un-*brrr*-lieveably fun, with plenty of pond hockey, ice-skating, skiing, snowmobiling, ice fishing, and, of course, messy piles of hot chicken wings. The Erie Canal was extremely important to the city's growth, and today Canalside is the center of its waterfront action. So pull on your mittens and lace up your skates! We're going for a glide.

Wave a pussy willow branch in one of the nation's largest DYNGUS DAY parades, celebrating the springtime Polish American holiday. Butter lambs are another springtime tradition.

In 1910, the Albright-Knox Art Gallery in Buffalo was the first museum in the United States to host an exhibit featuring PHOTOGRAPHY as a fine art. Find it today as the Buffalo AKG Art Museum.

Heyy-eyy-eyy-eyy! In BUFFALO BILLS country, everyone greets you with "Go Bills," and car horns beep to the tune of "Let's Go Buffalo."

Lunchtime! BEEF ON WECK, thinly sliced roast beef piled on a freshly baked kummelweck roll, is the classic Buffalo sandwich. Quench your thirst with a dark-red LOGANBERRY drink. A loganberry is a cross between a raspberry and a blackberry.

The Awe of Mother Nature

New York experiences some weirdly wild weather, especially when it comes to rain and snow and snow and, well, even more snow. The state also rocks the most incredible natural wonders, including countless cool caves, canyons, and caverns.

Shake, Rattle, and Crack

The state's strongest recorded EARTHQUAKE—5.9 on the Richter scale—shook Massena on September 5, 1944, but was felt as far away as Maryland and Maine.

The Ellenville Fault Ice Caves contain the nation's largest-known exposed FAULT SYSTEM. A fault is a fracture, or crack, in Earth's crust.

Snow Problem

Who will take home the GOLDEN SNOWBALL AWARD? Every year, Albany, Binghamton, Buffalo, Rochester, and Syracuse compete to be named snowiest upstate city. Each can average more than eight feet of the white stuff!

LAKE EFFECT SNOW, which happens when cold air passes over the warmer waters of a not-yet-frozen lake (we're looking at you, Lake Ontario and Lake Erie!), is responsible for much of the powder pileup.

Brrrr! Old Forge recorded the state's LOWEST TEMPERATURE—a numbing 52 degrees below zero in 1979!

New York has dug itself out of some epic 24-HOUR SNOWFALLS: about 49 inches in Watertown (1900), 54 inches in Montague (1976), 51 inches in Barnes Corners (1997). Barnes Corners lies on the Tug Hill Plateau, one of the snowiest spots in the Northeast.

And the Rain Poured Down

During Tropical Storm Henri in 2021, Islip got deluged with 11 inches of RAIN in just two hours!

When Hurricane Sandy blew into the southern part of the state in 2012, wicked wind gusts and record-high tides FLOODED the NYC subway system, and the nation's stock exchanges shut down for multiple days.

NOR'EASTERS are no joke. The intense cyclone-like storms with winds from the northeast (which explains their name) bring a stunning amount of rain or snow and flooding.

Natural Wonders

Inside a small grotto in Chestnut Ridge Park is ETERNAL FLAME FALLS, a small waterfall where a natural gas spring has kept a flame flickering for what's believed to be thousands of years.

Bubbles! Some people think that the naturally carbonated water from SARATOGA SPRINGS' underground mineral springs has healing powers.

In 1842, farmer Lester Howe noticed a stream of cold air rising from a hole in his field. When he climbed in to investigate, he discovered miles of underground caves filled with huge stalagmites and stalactites! Today you can take a boat ride on the underground lake through HOWE CAVERNS, the largest cavern in the Northeast.

HUDSON CANYON, located southeast of NYC, is the largest underwater canyon in the U.S. portion of the Atlantic Ocean. You could stack seven Empire State Buildings from the seafloor to the surface!

Close Encounters

In 1992, a 27-pound METEORITE estimated to be 4.4 billion years old hit a parked car in Peekskill. In 2020, another large meteorite exploded and disintegrated in the air above Syracuse, creating a sonic boom heard all over Central New York. Thankfully, no one was hurt by either space rock.

Niagara Falls

Wow! Do you hear the tremendous rush of thundering water? Straddling the New York–Canada border, Niagara Falls is the world's fastest-moving waterfall. More than 700,000 gallons of water per second pour over Niagara Falls at about 25 miles per hour. To help understand its intensity— that much water can fill an Olympic-sized swimming pool in half a second, or faster than the blink of an eye. We sure don't want to *mist* this magnificent natural wonder!

Spin cycle! When the huge volume of rushing water reaches the narrow Great Gorge, it forms a swirling vortex or WHIRLPOOL, leading to some of the world's most EXTREME RAPIDS.

In 1859, French circus performer Charles Blondin became the first to TIGHTROPE WALK across the Niagara Gorge. In 1876, Maria Spelterini became the first woman to cross on a tightrope. Both daredevils later crossed the gorge blindfolded!

Niagara Falls is made up of THREE WATERFALLS: American Falls and Bridal Veil Falls (both on the U.S. side) and Horseshoe Falls (almost entirely on the Canadian side).

Go with the flow! Walk under the rushing water at the CAVE OF THE WINDS. The cave collapsed in the early 1900s, but the name is still used for the wooden decks at the base of the Falls.

Passengers on the MAID OF THE MIST wear ponchos to keep dry as they travel under the cascading Falls. The original boat's maiden, or first, voyage was in 1846.

Niagara Falls was created when GLACIERS from the Ice Age melted around 12,000 years ago.

Niagara Falls is the nation's OLDEST STATE PARK (1885).

The clock is ticking. The Falls have been ERODING at about one foot per year. Scientists speculate that in 2,000 years, the American Falls section could dry up.

RAINBOWS are often seen on sunny days. They're caused by sunlight streaming through the mist created by the falling water.

Walk, drive, or bike over RAINBOW BRIDGE, and you're in Canada.

In the 1890s, Nikola Tesla and George Westinghouse designed the world's first HYDROELECTRIC POWER PLANT in Niagara Falls. (*Hydro* means "water.") Today, the American side of the Falls can generate enough electricity to light 24 million light bulbs at the same time.

Of the FISH that plummet over the falls, some 90 percent survive, possibly because the foam at the bottom cushions their landing.

A barrel of fun? On her 63rd birthday in 1901, schoolteacher Annie Edson Taylor became the first-known person to survive going over the falls in a BARREL. Thousands of daredevils have since tried the same feat, and fewer than twenty have lived.

Weird, Weirder, Weirdest

New York can be super weird when it wants to be, and sometimes fabulous stuff doesn't neatly fit into one category. But that's the definition of unique New York, right? So we've gathered the oddness together!

The marble LIONS guarding the New York Public Library in Bryant Park, NYC, are named Patience and Fortitude.

The colors on the CAMPBELL'S SOUP CAN came about after an employee attended a Cornell University football game in 1898 and loved the red-and-white uniforms so much.

Dr. William R. Brooks, professor of astronomy at Hobart College in Geneva, discovered over 27 COMETS between 1881 and 1912. Most discoveries were made using telescopes he created himself.

The high-kickin' Rockettes perform every holiday season at Radio City Music Hall, the world's LARGEST INDOOR THEATER with the world's largest stage curtain.

Albert Einstein's EYEBALLS are stored in a safe-deposit box in NYC.

There's a CHEESE VENDING MACHINE in Perry and a BACON VENDING MACHINE in Warrensburg!

Easiest zip code ever! The zip code for the huge General Electric plant in Schenectady is 12345. Every year, thousands of kids mistakenly send letters for Santa here. A better bet would be NORTH POLE, a small town in the foothills of Whiteface Mountain.

In Saratoga Springs, Christmas is celebrated by smashing a candy PEPPERMINT PIG with a tiny hammer.

There's a painted pig rock in Speculator and an elephant rock in Hague—the ultimate PET ROCKS!

Three-across and five-down. The first-ever CROSSWORD PUZZLE, called a word-cross, was published in the *New York World* newspaper in 1913.

Click your heels and follow the YELLOW-BRICK SIDEWALKS in Chittenango, home of L. Frank Baum, author of *The Wonderful Wizard of Oz*.

Meet me at the clock! The FOUR-FACED CLOCK in the center of Grand Central Terminal in NYC sits on top of an info booth that has a secret spiral staircase leading to the train station's lower level.

Cross Island Chapel, in the middle of an Oneida pond, claims to be the world's SMALLEST CHURCH. Only three people can fit inside!

Legend in Lyndonville says if you make a wish, tie your laces together, then toss your shoes up into one of the town's SHOE TREES, your wish will come true (but only if your shoes catch a branch).

The lower deck of the George Washington Bridge, connecting NYC with New Jersey, is nicknamed MARTHA, after the president's wife.

There's a lot of BIG statues and stuff in New York:
Button and Needle—NYC
Cow—Lowville
Crows—Omar
Duck—Flanders
Garden Gnome—Kerhonkson
Painted Shamrock—Oyster Bay
Pair of Pants—Homer
Pepsi-Cola Sign—Long Island City
Roll of Life Savers—Gouverneur
Totem Pole—Cooperstown

A TREE grows up through Hoss's Country Corner in Long Lake and out the roof!

Index

Major League Professional Sports Teams

National Football League
Buffalo Bills, New York Giants*, New York Jets*
Major League Baseball
New York Mets, New York Yankees
National Basketball Association
Brooklyn Nets, New York Knicks
Women's National Basketball Association
New York Liberty
Major League Soccer
New York City FC, New York Red Bulls*
National Women's Soccer League
NJ/NY Gotham FC*
National Hockey League
Buffalo Sabres, New York Islanders, New York Rangers
Premier Hockey Federation
Buffalo Beauts

* The Giants, Jets, Red Bulls, and Gotham play in New Jersey and represent the New York metropolitan area.